SPORTS GREATS
TOP 10
CRAZIEST PLAYS
IN FOOTBALL

DAVID ARETHA

E **Enslow Publishing**
101 W. 23rd Street
Suite 240
New York, NY 10011
USA

enslow.com

Published in 2017 by Enslow Publishing, LLC.
101 W. 23rd Street, Suite 240, New York, NY 10011

Library of Congress Cataloging-in-Publication Data

Names: Aretha, David, author.
Title: Top 10 craziest plays in football / David Aretha.
Other titles: Top ten craziest plays in football
Description: New York : Enslow Publishing, LLC, 2017 | Series: Sports greats | Includes bibliographical references and index.
Identifiers: LCCN 2016022707| ISBN 9780766083066 (Library Bound) | ISBN 9780766083042 (Paperback) | ISBN 9780766083059 (6-pack)
Subjects: LCSH: Football—United States—History—Juvenile literature. | Football—United States—Miscellanea—Juvenile literature.
Classification: LCC GV950.7 .A7899 2017 | DDC 796.330973—dc23
LC record available at https://lccn.loc.gov/2016022707

Printed in China

To Our Readers: We have done our best to make sure all website addresses in this book were active and appropriate when we went to press. However, the author and the publisher have no control over and assume no liability for the material available on those websites or on any websites they may link to. Any comments or suggestions can be sent by e-mail to customerservice@enslow.com.

Photos Credits: Cover, pp. 1, 21 Allen Kee/Getty Images Sport/Getty Images; p. 4 AP Photo/Tomasso DeRosa; pp. 9, 27, 29, 35, 37, 41, 43, 45 © AP Images; p. 11 Dick Raphael/Sports Illustrated/Getty Images; p. 12 AP Photo/NFL Photos; p. 15 Focus on Sport/Getty Images; p. 17 AP Photo/San Diego Union/Thane McIntosh; p. 19 Joe Robbins/Getty Images Sport/Getty Images; p. 23 Al Messerschmidt/Getty Images Sport/Getty Images; p. 25 Jamie Squire/Getty Images Sport/Getty Images; pp. 31, 33 Heinz Kluetmeier/Sports Illustrated/Getty Images; p. 39 Rey Del Rio/Getty Images Sport/Getty Images; design elements throughout book: maodoltee/Shutterstock.com (football field), RTimages/Shutterstock.com (grass), EsraKeskinSenay/Shutterstock.com (football stadium), Prixel Creative/Shutterstock.com (football play).

CONTENTS

INTRODUCTION

Andre Parker, a linebacker for Kent State, made a big "oops!" play in the 2012 season opener.

H ave your parents ever gone the wrong way on the expressway? Did they ever, say, get on I-75 South when they should have been on I-75 North? And they kept driving for miles, yearning for the next exit ramp, as everyone in the car got increasingly frustrated and tense?

That is kind of like what happed to Roy Riegels on January 1, 1929. Only it happened on a football field.

In the Rose Bowl against Georgia Tech, Riegels committed his infamous wrong-way run. An outstanding center for the University of California, Riegels screwed up royally in this game against Georgia Tech. After recovering a teammate's fumble near the sideline, Riegels ran five yards in the right direction and then made a complete U-turn. He then ran 69 yards in the *wrong* direction.

Teammate Benny Lom ran after Riegels, screaming at him to stop. "Get away from me," Riegels replied. "This is my touchdown." Georgia Tech coach Bill Alexander loved it. "Every step he takes is to our advantage," he told his players. Lom finally caught up with Riegels at the 3-yard line and turned him around. Defenders then tackled him near the goal line. Georgia Tech proceeded to block Cal's punt, and they recovered it for a safety. That gave Georgia Tech a 2–0 lead in the second quarter.

The play seems funny now, but it wasn't to Riegels at the time. He didn't want to return to the field in the second half. "Coach, I can't do it," he said. "I've ruined you, I've ruined myself, I've ruined the University of California. I couldn't face that crowd to save my life."

Riegels returned, but his team lost, 8–7. If he hadn't run the wrong way, Cal likely would have won the game.

Thanks to YouTube, Riegels's run can be seen easily at any time. So can that of Andre Parker, a Kent State linebacker. Against Towson University in 2012, Kent State punted the ball to the 7-yard line. Parker was supposed to just down the ball. But for some reason, he returned the ball the other way. Parker ran 64 yards toward his own end zone. Equally perplexing, Towson players pursued him and knocked him out of bounds. As he walked off the field, Parker realized his mistake and hung his head. Luckily for him, a player on a punting team can't return the ball. It was placed back on the 7-yard line.

These are two of the worst football blunders ever, but not the weirdest. It's time to take a break from the seriousness of your day and enjoy the 10 craziest plays in football history.

WRONG-WAY RUN

KEY PLAYER: JIM MARSHALL

TEAM: MINNESOTA VIKINGS

OPPONENT: SAN FRANCISCO 49ERS

SETTING: SAN FRANCISCO, CALIFORNIA, OCTOBER 25, 1964

In his twenty-one-year career, Jim Marshall recovered thirty fumbles — a feat that remains an NFL record. Unfortunately, it was one too many. The same could be said about his 270 consecutive starts with the Minnesota Vikings, which set a league record. People seem to talk about only one of those games — the one in which he returned a fumble to the wrong end zone.

"As far as I'm concerned, it's the all-time [blunder]," said Fred Cox, the Vikings' kicker at the time. "Who could conceive of a guy picking up the ball and running the wrong way?"

Jim Marshall happened to be a great player. He was one of the "Purple People Eaters," Minnesota's legendary defensive line. He stood six feet four inches (193 centimeters), weighed 240 pounds (109 kilograms), and started every game for almost twenty straight seasons. "He's just one of those people who has been blessed with a great body," Vikings trainer Fred Zamberletti told *Sports Illustrated*. Marshall is a caring man, too. He has worked with scholarship funds to help send inner-city kids to college, and he helped establish a transportation company for senior citizens and the physically challenged.

Some say he would have made the Pro Football Hall of Fame...if it weren't for that one play.

Ironically, Marshall had made a terrific play just minutes earlier. It was the fourth quarter at Kezar Stadium in San Francisco. Minnesota was leading 20–17 when Marshall hit 49ers quarterback George Mira, forcing a fumble. Carl Eller picked up the ball and ran 45 yards for a touchdown.

Now trailing 27–17, the 49ers were desperate to score. Mira fired a pass to Billy Kilmer around San Francisco's 27-yard line. Kilmer plowed forward a few more yards and then Minnesota's Karl Kassulke knocked the ball out of his hands. Marshall picked up the ball and ran 66 yards to the end zone—the *wrong* end zone.

"I was like everybody else on the sideline," Vikings backup quarterback Ron Vander Kelen told TwinCities .com. "We were yelling, 'You're going the wrong way! You're going the wrong way!'"

For Marshall, it was the easiest "touchdown" of his life. A couple times he looked back and saw no 49ers on his tail. He trotted into the end zone and then flipped the ball toward the sidelines. That constituted a safety—two points for San Francisco. Seconds later, as fans were cheering and laughing, Marshall realized what he had done. The 49ers' Bruce Bosley patted him on the back, and then Marshall bent over in despair.

Vikings head coach Norm Van Brocklin typically scolded players for making mistakes. But in this case, he realized that yelling at Marshall would serve no purpose. Marshall recalled to TwinCities.com: "He just said, 'Hey, Jim, just forget about it.' And that's what I remember and that's what I've been trying to do."

Jim Marshall looks around and sees no 49ers trying to stop him. Wonder why!

Fortunately for the Vikings, they hung on to win the game, 27–22. When the team arrived in Minneapolis later that night, Marshall told the press, "All the guys on the plane asked me to take over as pilot. They figured I'd land them in Hawaii."

Later, Marshall received a letter from Roy Riegels, who had run the wrong way in the 1929 Rose Bowl. "Welcome to the club!" Riegels wrote.

IMMACULATE RECEPTION
KEY PLAYER: FRANCO HARRIS
TEAM: PITTSBURGH STEELERS
OPPONENT: OAKLAND RAIDERS
SETTING: PITTSBURGH, PENNSYLVANIA, DECEMBER 23, 1972

With 22 seconds to go in the Steelers' play-off game, team owner Art Rooney stopped watching. He took the elevator down to field level, where he planned to comfort his players following another failed season.

Art Rooney was football's lovable loser. The kind-hearted cigar smoker had owned the Steelers since 1933, and never had they won a play-off game. This looked like another loss, too. Oakland quarterback Ken Stabler had romped 30 yards for a touchdown with 1:13 left, to give the Raiders a 7–6 lead. Now the Steelers were in a desperate situation. They faced fourth down at their own 40-yard line with 22 ticks remaining. But as Rooney took his elevator ride, something amazing happened: the "Immaculate Reception."

Quarterback Terry Bradshaw, the fun-loving country boy from Louisiana, lined up behind center. In front of him was the nastiest defense in football. The black-and-silver Raiders hit ferociously and didn't always play within the rules. Safety Jack "the Assassin" Tatum would one day hit a wide receiver so hard, the player would spend the rest of his life in a wheelchair.

Soon after Bradshaw took the snap, he was in deep trouble. Nobody was open, and defensive ends Horace

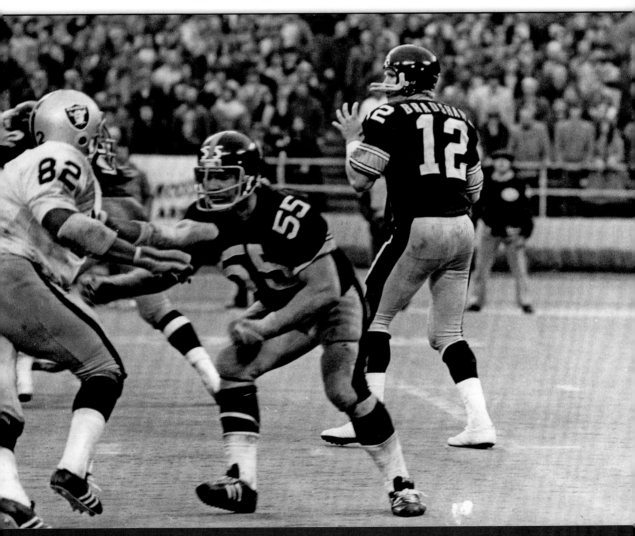

Terry Bradshaw struggled against the nasty Raiders defense all

Jones and Tony Cline converged on him. Bradshaw had to scramble out of the pocket, but as he did he nearly tripped over one of his blockers. Finally, with Jones and Cline still breathing down his throat, Bradshaw rifled the ball downfield.

Running back John Fuqua rose to make the catch at the Oakland 35-yard line. But as soon as the ball arrived, Tatum smashed into him like a Mack truck. The ball ricocheted off Tatum, Fuqua, or both of them and went backward—to around the Oakland 42-yard line. Raiders defensive back Jimmy Warren raised his arms in victory,

After Terry Bradshaw's pass ricocheted off the receiver (or defender), everyone thought the ball was incomplete. But not Franco Harris. He grabbed the ball before it hit the ground and then ran it in for a touchdown.

but the play wasn't over. Before the ball could fall to the ground incomplete, Steelers rookie running back Franco Harris grabbed it inches above the ground. Harris took off down the left sideline, flicked away Warren at the 10, and stormed into the end zone!

Steelers fans went bananas, jumping up and down and pumping their fists. Some leaped over Three Rivers Stadium's high wall and mobbed Harris in the end zone. "You talk about Christmas miracles," Curt Gowdy blared on the NBC telecast. "Here's the miracle of all miracles."

While the Steelers celebrated the Immaculate Reception, the Raiders claimed that it shouldn't have been allowed. NFL rules stated that if an offensive player caught a ball that had caromed off a teammate, it was not a completion. However, the referees could not determine that the ball had hit Fuqua; it might have just hit Tatum. So the call stood, and Pittsburgh won its first-ever play-off game, 13–7.

To this day, the Immaculate Reception remains one of the most famous plays in NFL history. Though the Steelers lost the next week to Miami, they went on to dominate the decade. Art Rooney celebrated Super Bowl victories following the 1975, 1976, 1978, and 1979 seasons.

In Pittsburgh, the legend of the Immaculate Reception has never diminished. In fact, Harris said, the "play just gets bigger every year."

HOLY ROLLER

KEY PLAYER: DAVE CASPER
TEAM: OAKLAND RAIDERS
OPPONENT: SAN DIEGO CHARGERS
SETTING: SAN DIEGO, CALIFORNIA, SEPTEMBER 10, 1978

The San Diego Chicken, the famous mascot, couldn't believe it. The visiting Oakland Raiders had just scored the craziest game-winning touchdown anyone had ever seen. The Chicken fell on the ground at San Diego Stadium and lay motionless. He looked as though he had just suffered a deadly heart attack. All throughout the stadium, San Diego fans were equally shocked.

"The Chargers are standing, looking at each other, looking at the sky!" cried Raiders radio broadcaster Bill King. "They don't believe it! Nobody believes it! I don't know if the Raiders believe it! It's not real!"

Oh, the "Holy Roller" play was real all right. But bizarre.

The game took place on a sunny September afternoon in 1978. San Diego led, 20–14, with just 10 seconds remaining, but the home fans were nervous.

Oakland's Ken Stabler was about to be sacked to end the game. But then he decided to roll the ball forward.

Oakland had the ball at the Chargers' 14-yard line. A Raiders touchdown would tie the game, and an extra point would win it.

Oakland quarterback Ken Stabler broke the huddle. In high school, Stabler had earned the nickname "the Snake" after one of his great runs. But now, at age thirty-two, he was slow on his feet for an NFL quarterback. After taking the snap on this play, Stabler dropped back to pass. Not finding anyone open—and facing a heavy rush—he kept backpedaling. When linebacker Woodrow Lowe wrapped his arms around the quarterback, the Snake appeared to be doomed. While being tackled at the 24, Stabler desperately underhanded the ball forward.

The fumble hit at the 17-yard line and bounced like a basketball to the 13. There, running back Pete Banaszak got his hands on it. Banaszak was about to be tackled, so he, too, flipped the ball forward. Tight end Dave Casper reached for the ball. Stumbling forward, Casper batted the ball at the 5 and then again at the 2. He then fell on his face just past the goal line—with the ball under his chest. He cradled it like a baby for a touchdown.

That's when the Chicken died.

"The Raiders have won the football game!" King blared. "Fifty-two thousand people...are stunned!"

The Chargers refused to accept defeat. They argued that it was against the rules to intentionally fumble a football forward. The officials declared that it was not apparent that the Raiders had intentionally fumbled the ball. Apparently, the ball had simply floated and bounced 25 yards in a direction that favored the Raiders! Their ruling was final, and Errol Mann kicked the game-winning extra point.

After the contest, Stabler admitted, "I fumbled it on purpose." Banaszak and Casper also said they had tried to bat the ball toward the goal line. Those admissions just made Chargers fans even madder.

After the season, the NFL changed the rules. On fourth down or in the last two minutes of a game, a player could not fumble the ball forward to a teammate. The ball would be ruled down at the spot of the fumble. For Stabler, that would have been the 24-yard line if the rule had been in place that day.

Oakland tight end Dave Casper stumbles, bumbles, and fumbles into the end zone, where he would fall on the ball for the game-winning touchdown.

"Now," King concluded, "this one will be relived forever—bitterly here in San Diego, joyfully in Oakland. Final score: Oakland 21, San Diego 20.

MUSIC CITY MIRACLE
KEY PLAYER: KEVIN DYSON
TEAM: TENNESSEE TITANS
OPPONENT: BUFFALO BILLS
SETTING: NASHVILLE, TENNESSEE, JANUARY 8, 2000

"Do the Titans have a miracle left in them?" asked Tennessee Titans radio broadcaster Mike Keith. "If they do, they need it now."

By "now," Keith meant at the very end of Tennessee's wild-card play-off game on January 8, 2000. The Titans trailed Buffalo, 16–15, with 16 seconds remaining in Nashville, Tennessee, also known as Music City.

The Titans were about to receive a kickoff. Did they have a miracle left in them? Tennessee safety Blaine Bishop didn't think so. "The first thing I thought after that kick is, 'Where am I going for vacation? The season's over,'" he told the *Buffalo News*.

The Titans were not used to such situations. Three years earlier, the team moved from Houston to Nashville. They went 8–8 in both 1997 and 1998, but then 13–3 under head coach Jeff Fisher in 1999.

Six-foot-three (190 cm) running back Eddie George rushed for 1,304 yards that year. Defensive end Jevon Kearse led the defense with 14.5 sacks. But in the final two minutes, it all came down to the special teams. With 1:48 remaining, Al Del Greco booted a wobbly 36-yard field goal to put Tennessee ahead, 15–13. Then Stevie Christie gave the Bills a 16–15 lead with a 41-yard field goal with 0:16 remaining. Now came the kickoff.

Titans special teams coordinator Alan Lowry had a kickoff-return play called the Home Run Throwback. The Titans practiced the play every

When Stevie Christie kicked his field goal with 16 seconds remaining, he thought it was a game winner. But Buffalo's 16–15 lead would soon vanish.

week, but they never used it. Now, they were about to use it.

Christie pooch kicked the ball to Tennessee's 25-yard line. Fullback Lorenzo Neal caught the ball, which was a minor miracle in itself. Neal had earned the nickname "Spoons" for his slippery hands. But he caught this one and ran a few steps to his right. He then handed the ball to Frank Wycheck, a tight end who used to be a catcher on his high school baseball team. He had a good throwing arm.

Wycheck also ran to his right, drawing the Bills toward that side of the field. Then came the trickery. Wycheck stopped and fired the ball to the far left of the field, right to wide receiver Kevin Dyson.

Dyson had almost a clear path down the left sideline. "There was a brief moment in there when I thought, 'Get out of bounds. Kick the field goal to win,'" Dyson told the *Buffalo News*. "But when Steve Christie fell down, it was smooth sailing from there."

With blockers on his right side, Dyson raced untouched toward the end zone. "Twenty! Ten! Five! Touchdown, Titans!" Keith screamed. "There are no flags on the field! It's a miracle!"

However, the officials almost took the miracle away. Replays indicated that Wycheck's pass to Dyson may have gone forward, not backward, which is not allowed on a kick return. The refs could not determine that for certain, so they left the play as is. The Titans won, 22–16, then rode their magic to two road play-off wins. Only in the Super Bowl did they run out of steam, losing to the St. Louis Rams, 23–16.

While the Titans remember the play as miraculous, Bills fans refer to it as cursed. Since that game, Buffalo has gone through eight head coaches and has yet to make the play-offs.

Tennessee's Kevin Dyson scores on the kickoff return to complete the miracle. Three weeks later, Dyson would be tackled one yard short of the St. Louis goal line on the last play of the Super Bowl, a 23–16 loss for the Titans.

RIVER CITY RELAY

Key Player: Jerome Pathon

Team: New Orleans Saints

Opponent: Jacksonville Jaguars

Setting: Jacksonville, Florida, December 21, 2003

T he Saints were utterly desperate. With a record of 7–7, they needed to beat the Jaguars to have a chance to make the play-offs. But with seven seconds left against Jacksonville, the Saints trailed, 20–13, and were on their own 25-yard line. Not even a Hail Mary pass would work since the goal line was too far away for a long throw. No, they needed something more powerful than a Hail Mary. They needed "All Go Special."

On a sunlit field, quarterback Aaron Brooks set up in shotgun formation. Three men lined up as receivers on the left side, including running back Deuce McAllister. Deuce rushed for a whopping 1,641 yards that year and also caught 69 passes. Wide receiver Donte' Stallworth lined up on the right side. He averaged an impressive 19.4 yards per catch in 2003, but the Saints now needed 75.

Brooks snapped the ball, and "All Go Special" began. Brooks scanned the field and then lateralled to

Stallworth at the 50-yard line near the right sideline. Stallworth broke two tackles and then raced toward the middle of the field. Around the 33-yard line, he faced a couple tacklers, so he pitched the ball back to Michael Lewis. Lewis ran toward the left sideline, where he faced more Jaguars, so he handed the ball back to McAllister. He ran five yards before being sandwiched by two defenders. Before going down, he lateralled the ball to the middle of the field—into the hands of wide receiver

The Saints' Jerome Pathon caught a lateral toss mid-stride and sprinted toward the goal line. Though no tacklers were nearby, he dove into the end zone.

Jerome Pathon. Pathon grabbed it at the 23 and sprinted toward the goal line. Out of pure excitement, he dove into the empty end zone.

Saints radio broadcaster Hokie Gajan couldn't believe it. "You can't tell me...what I just witnessed... took place!" he said.

"Merry Christmas, everybody!" added Gajan's radio partner Jim Henderson. "Merrrrrry Christmas!"

The Saints had just executed a nearly impossible play. Now they just needed to kick the extra point to tie the game. Easy-peasy, right? After all, NFL kickers successfully converted extra points more than 99 percent of the time. Saints kicker John Carney had made 131 consecutive extra points up to this moment. Earlier in the year, Saints head coach Jim Haslett had said, "If I had my life riding on a kick, I'd have John Carney out there."

For Carney, the conditions for the kick were perfect—the weather, the snap, and the hold. But he missed it.

"Noooooo!" screamed Gajan.

"He missed the extra point, wide right!" Henderson blared. "How could he do that?!"

The "All Go Special" had been followed by "Oh No Carney." Elation followed by despair.

"Nothing in the NFL is a foregone conclusion, but c'mon, that's a foregone conclusion," said Saints tight end Walter Rasby.

With the loss, New Orleans was officially eliminated from the play-offs. Afterward, the veteran Carney patiently answered the media's questions.

"Utter shock—that's a good way to put it," he said. "I can't believe it myself. As far as kickers are concerned, that's as bad as it gets."

Donte' Stallworth lies down in exhaustion after the stunning touchdown. Stallworth caught the pass, survived a hit, broke a tackle, and made a great move before flipping the first lateral.

THE BIG BAND PLAY
KEY PLAYER: KEVIN MOEN
TEAM: CALIFORNIA BEARS
OPPONENT: STANFORD CARDINAL
SETTING: BERKELEY, CALIFORNIA, NOVEMBER 20, 1982

After "the Play," Cal announcer Joe Starkey went berserk. "The Bears have won! The Bears have won!" he screamed. "The most amazing, sensational, dramatic, heart-rending...exciting, thrilling finish in the history of college football! California has won the Big Game over Stanford!"

Sometimes football announcers get overly excited and start exaggerating. But this really was the most dramatic and thrilling finish in football history. Even before "the Play" occurred, it had already been an amazing game.

The Cal Bears hosted the Stanford Cardinal, their big rival since 1892. If Stanford could win, they likely would go to a bowl game. Legendary Stanford quarterback John Elway did his best to make that happen. Down 19–17 late in the game, the Cardinal

Stanford band members, thinking the game is over, storm the field. Soon they'll realize that Cal players still have the ball and are coming their way!

faced a fourth-and-17 at their own 13-yard line. Elway came through with a 29-yard pass completion, and Stanford later kicked a field goal to go up, 20–19. "Only a miracle can save the Bears now," Starkey declared.

Stanford's excessive celebration resulted in a 15-yard penalty. So, with four seconds left, the Cardinal kicked off from their 25-yard line (instead of the 40). "The Play" started with only twenty-one men on the field because Cal was a player short. It ended with over one hundred men—and women—on the field.

"The Play" began when Stanford's kicker booted the ball to Cal's 45. Kevin Moen caught it and soon lateralled to Richard Rodgers. Rodgers found no running room and lateralled to Dwight Garner—still on the Cal

45. Garner ran five yards and was surrounded by five Stanford defenders. Thinking Garner had been tackled, the Stanford band poured onto the field—right into the end zone that Cal was moving toward.

Meanwhile, Garner avoided being tackled and pitched the ball to Rodgers. Near the Stanford 45, Rodgers lateralled to Mariet Ford. At the 27, with the band now just a few yards ahead of him, Ford ran into three defenders. Blindly, he tossed the ball over his shoulder. Moen caught it at the 25 and ran through the band members for a touchdown!

Amid the chaos, Moen barreled over trombone player Gary Tyrrell in the end zone. "I thought I'd be famous for my talent as a musician, not for being knocked down at a football game," Tyrell said.

The officials were dumbfounded by the play. They didn't signal a touchdown. Some thought Garner's knee had hit the ground, which would have ended the play. Others thought that the fifth lateral, to Moen, had gone forward—which would have been illegal. The band's presence on the field had added to the chaos. Officials didn't have instant replay back then, so they couldn't review the play.

After much discussion, referee Charles Moffett addressed the Cal crowd. "There was dead silence in the place," Moffett recalled. "Then when I raised my arms [signaling a touchdown], I thought I had started World War III. It was like an atomic bomb had gone off."

More than seventy-five thousand fans erupted in joy. "The Bear would not quit," proclaimed Cal coach Joe Kapp. "The Bear would not die."

This unbelievable game is honored at the College Football Hall of Fame, where Gary Tyrrell's smashed trombone is on display.

Cal's Kevin Moen (*center*) and Keith Kartz (*right*) bask in glory after the madcap victory. It was Moen who plowed through the

FLUTIE'S FLING

KEY PLAYER: DOUG FLUTIE

TEAM: BOSTON COLLEGE GOLDEN EAGLES

OPPONENT: MIAMI HURRICANES

SETTING: MIAMI, FLORIDA, NOVEMBER 23, 1984

Doug Flutie stood only five feet nine inches (175 cm), which is extremely short for a quarterback. After all, how can a five-foot-nine QB see receivers down the field when the linemen are six-foot-four? Yet, the gutsy little quarterback loved to face challenges.

At Boston College, Flutie earned the starting quarterback job as a true freshman. He went on to become the first player in major college football to throw for 10,000 career yards. In 1984, he won the Heisman Trophy. And on November 23 of that year, he completed the most famous Hail Mary pass in college football history. "I've always enjoyed trying to figure out a way to come from behind, try to win," he told the *Washington Post*.

The son of an aerospace engineer, Flutie launched his rocket of a pass at the Orange Bowl in Miami. Before the historic ending, the University of Miami and Boston

Pint-sized quarterback Doug Flutie chucks the ball with all he's got on a Hail Mary pass for the ages. He had to throw the pigskin 63 yards into a stiff wind to reach the goal line.

College put on a spectacular offensive show. Miami's Bernie Kosar threw for a school-record 447 yards. Boston College led, 28–21, at halftime when a tropical storm arrived, adding drama to this thrilling battle.

The game was tied 31–31 entering the fourth quarter. With 3:50 left, Boston College scored a touchdown to go up, 41–38. Miami then overcame a third-and-21 and a fourth-and-1 before finding the end zone. With 28 seconds remaining, the Hurricanes led, 45–41.

"I assumed we had lost," BC coach Jack Bicknell said after the game. "I'm thinking, 'What am I going to tell these guys in the locker room?'"

Flutie, though, remained much more optimistic. "OK, let's get near midfield," he told his teammates, as he recalled to ESPN.com. "If we can get it there, we have a 50-50 chance of scoring."

Flutie completed a 19-yard pass to Troy Stradford and then a 13-yarder to Scott Gieselman. With six seconds remaining, BC had the ball on the Miami 48. Time for one more play.

A 50-50 chance of scoring? Hardly. Flutie called "Flood Tip," BC's version of the Hail Mary. Three wide receivers would race downfield, "flooding" an area of the end zone. Flutie would heave the ball toward his three receivers and hope one of them would catch it.

But Flutie was just a little guy. How could he pass it that far? And, due to the storm, he would have to throw the ball against a thirty-mile-per-hour wind! Impossible.

Flutie dropped back to pass, and immediately a defender got after him. Flutie then dropped back even farther. By the time he released his throw, he was standing on his own 37-yard line. And yet his pass sailed and sailed and sailed, until it was… "Caught by Boston College!" screamed CBS broadcaster Brent Musburger. "I don't believe it! It's a touchdown! The Eagles win it!"

Boston College players revel in victory following the Hail Mary pass. In the center of this photo, a teammate hoists heroic receiver Gerry Phelan on his shoulder.

The pass had cleared a wall of players and landed in the arms of receiver Gerry Phelan. Flutie— being so short and all—didn't see who caught it. But due to all the celebrating in the end zone, he knew his team had won. As Flutie pumped his fist in jubilation, a teammate lifted him up and carried him down the field. For a few exhilarating seconds, Flutie looked and felt like he was ten feet tall.

BAHAMA DRAMA

KEY PLAYER: TITUS DAVIS

TEAM: CENTRAL MICHIGAN CHIPPEWAS

OPPONENT: WESTERN KENTUCKY HILLTOPPERS

SETTING: NASSAU, BAHAMAS, DECEMBER 24, 2014

There are so many bowl games on TV during the holiday season that fans ignore the lesser ones. You know, like the Famous Idaho Potato Bowl and the San Diego County Credit Union Poinsettia Bowl. On Christmas Eve 2014, Central Michigan and Western Kentucky played in one of those games: the Popeyes Bahamas Bowl.

Few Michiganders and Kentuckians could afford to fly to the Bahamas, and Bahamians are not exactly huge football fans. So, attendance at Thomas Robinson Stadium was only 13,667. Though the game was aired on ESPN, few fans paid attention...until the fourth quarter. At that point, they put their Christmas festivities on hold.

Entering the final quarter, Western Kentucky led, 49–14. The odds of Central Michigan coming back to win this game were virtually zero. Only one team in major college football history had overcome a 35-point deficit to win. And no team had ever erased all of that deficit in the fourth quarter.

The Chippewas could have easily given up. It's hard to stay focused on football when you're in a tropical paradise and it's the day before Christmas. But, behind quarterback Cooper Rush, CMU refused to die.

With 11:37 remaining, Rush threw a 12-yard touchdown pass to Titus Davis, a future NFL receiver. At the 8:03 mark, Rush completed a 23-yard scoring toss to Davis. At 3:06 and then 1:09, Rush fired two more touchdown passes to give him six for the game — tying

Western Kentucky defensive back Prince Charles Iworah can't catch Central Michigan wide receiver Titus Davis as he sprints toward the goal line's pylon. CMU's 49–14 fourth-quarter deficit was now 49–48!

the record for the most in a bowl game. Incredibly, Central Michigan had cut the deficit to 49–42.

The Chippewas then forced Western Kentucky to punt, but the Hilltoppers weren't too concerned. After all, CMU would start its drive on its own 25-yard line with just one second on the clock. "Last chance. What are you gonna do?" asked ESPN broadcaster Steve Levy.

The Chippewas' only hope would be to complete a pass and then keep lateralling the ball to teammates. It's the most desperate play in football, and it virtually never works.

This time, it worked.

Rush dropped back to pass and then launched a bomb to the 30-yard line. Amid a sea of players, CMU's Jesse Kroll rose to make the catch. As he was about to be tackled, Kroll tossed the ball back to Deon Butler. Butler ran to the 15 and, while he was being tackled, threw it back to Courtney Williams. Almost immediately, Williams lateralled to Titus Davis in the middle of the field. The speedy receiver sprinted on a slant to the right corner of the field. Pursued by three defenders, Davis dove for the pylon. If he could touch the orange stick before he went out of bounds, it would be a touchdown. He did!

Davis's amazing effort helped Rush complete his record-breaking seventh touchdown pass. But, CMU still trailed 49–48. Feeling lucky, CMU decided to try a two-point conversion to win the game. Rush lobbed a high pass to six-foot-three Kroll in the right corner of the end zone, but defender Wonderful Terry knocked the ball away.

Western Kentucky had survived, but no one would ever forget the Chippewas' historic effort. "They showed the heart and spirit that this game is all about," said Hilltoppers coach Jeff Brohm. And, they had given fans something to talk about on Christmas Eve.

Western Kentucky defensive back Wonderful Terry disrupts a pass intended for wide receiver Jesse Kroll on the failed two-point conversion. This brilliant play allowed the Hilltoppers to escape with the victory.

BLUNDER PUNT
KEY PLAYER: JALEN WATTS-JACKSON
TEAM: MICHIGAN STATE SPARTANS
OPPONENT: MICHIGAN WOLVERINES
SETTING: ANN ARBOR, MICHIGAN, OCTOBER 17, 2015

Excitement for this game was sky-high. More than 111,000 fans packed the "Big House" in Ann Arbor to witness the most anticipated Michigan-Michigan State game in years. In fact, it was the most-watched college football game on ESPN ever for the month of October. Fans witnessed an exciting game, all right. The ending of this battle was so shocking that one fan suffered a heart attack.

The University of Michigan has won more games (925 through 2015) than any team in college football history. For decades, the Wolverines were the dominant team in the state. But in 2007, things began to change. Michigan running back Mike Hart referred to Michigan State as the Wolverines' "little brother." That demeaning comment offended MSU coach Mark Dantonio. This rivalry "is not over," Dantonio said when responding to the quote. "I'm going to be a coach here for a long time. It's not over. It's just starting."

Soon, the fortunes of the two teams changed. Michigan State went 68–31 from 2008 to 2014, while the Wolverines were just 46–42. Michigan responded in 2015 by hiring head coach Jim Harbaugh. An all-American quarterback for Michigan in the 1980s, Harbaugh rose to become one of the NFL's top coaches. The intense Harbaugh immediately turned the Wolverines into a national power. Fans were so grateful that they started calling their city "Ann Harbaugh."

Entering this game, the Wolverines were 5–1. They had won their last three games 31–0, 28–0, and

Michigan's Blake O'Neill booted an 80-yard punt earlier in the contest. However, his bobble and scoop to MSU's Jalen Watts-Jackson (20) cost Michigan the game.

38–0. Michigan State was 6–0. The winner of this battle would contend for the national play-offs.

For most of the game, the Wolverines looked like they would win. They never trailed, and with nine minutes to go they led, 23–14. The Spartans then scored to cut the lead to 23–21. That's how it remained until 10 seconds were left on the clock. At that moment, ESPN estimated that MSU had only a one in five hundred chance of winning.

At 0:10, Michigan faced fourth-and-two at MSU's 47-yard line. Harbaugh called time-out and decided to punt the ball. Blake O'Neill, a former rugby player in Australia, was one of the best punters in the country. But on this play he didn't punt the ball.

The snap to O'Neill was perfect, but the ball bounced off his hands as if they were made of stone. O'Neill ran forward and picked up the ball, spun, and then—for some reason—flung the ball toward the sideline. "It's picked up by Michigan State's Jalen Watts-Jackson!" blared ESPN broadcaster Sean McDonough.

Watts-Jackson had never touched a football in a college game, but now he raced with the ball down the sideline. Michigan's Louis Grodman pursued him, but Watts-Jackson had a horde of blockers. "He scorrrrres!" McDonough screeched. "On the last play of the game! Unbelievable!"

So many MSU players piled on Watts-Jackson that he fractured his hip. Throughout the stadium, fans looked like they had witnessed a nuclear explosion. Harbaugh appeared sick. One fan performed CPR on the man who had suffered the heart attack.

"That's why football is loved so much in America," said a cheery Dantonio after the game. "It's because things like this happen."

The Spartans did indeed make the play-offs that season, but Alabama blew them out, 38–0. In Ann Harbaugh, no tears were shed.

Teammates pounce on Jalen Watts-Jackson after the shocking touchdown. The hero dislocated and fractured his left hip during the celebration, ending his season.

HALLOWEEN HORRORS

KEY PLAYER: CORN ELDER

TEAM: MIAMI HURRICANES

OPPONENT: DUKE BLUE DEVILS

SETTING: DURHAM, NORTH CAROLINA, OCTOBER 31, 2015

All excited and talking fast, University of Miami coach Larry Scott discussed the craziness he had just witnessed. "That was just like the old 'hot potato' game," he said. You know, the game where everyone tosses a ball or other object as quickly as possible to someone else. In this case, the players were Miami Hurricanes and the "potato" was a football.

Miami defeated Duke University, 30–27, on Halloween 2015, with an unbelievable eight-lateral kickoff return. The Hurricanes were suddenly euphoric following a horrific week for them.

The previous Saturday, Miami had suffered its worst defeat in history, 58–0 to Clemson. It was so bad that the school fired head coach Al Golden the next day. They promoted tight ends coach Larry Scott to interim head coach. Also during the week, the mother of cornerback Artie Burns had died. He promised to play the Duke game in her memory.

Due to the coaching turmoil, it was hard to get a game plan in place for the Duke game. "We used a joke earlier in the week about it being like a playground, about it being kind of like recess," Scott said. "And you know what? How about that? That's what it kind of turned into—a kids' game."

Miami's Dallas Crawford threw the play's first lateral pass and the last. Here he cuts upfield during the second time he had the ball, before pitching to Corn Elder.

The Hurricanes were so undisciplined during this game that they committed 23 penalties. They led, 24–12, late in the fourth quarter, but Duke scored touchdowns with 2:40 and 0:06 remaining to go up, 27–24. While fans in cozy Wallace Wade Stadium celebrated a certain victory, the Hurricanes contemplated another painful loss.

And then it happened—one of the wildest plays in football history. Over a period of 49 seconds, the following ensued: Dallas Crawford received the kickoff on the 25-yard line. He quickly ran into a wall of Blue Devils at the 30 and fired the ball back to Corn Elder at the 22. Elder jigged and jagged for a while and pitched a long pass that bounced to Jaquan Johnson. Johnson ran laterally and tossed it back to Mark Walton at the 15. Walton weaved through traffic and lateralled to Johnson.

Johnson seemed to say, "I don't want it," and immediately flipped it back to Tyre Brady. Brady threw it back to Elder at the 10. Elder threw a long lateral to Dallas Crawford (remember him?) at the 3. Crawford ran up the right sideline and cut to the middle. He then threw to Corn Elder at the 9-yard line near the left sideline. Elder then raced 91 yards for a touchdown, weaving through four tired Blue Devils along the way.

"You know...we just wanted to keep the ball alive...," Elder said. "We had a bunch of playmakers, and we made a play."

Although the clock said 0:00, the game still wasn't over. Officials needed nine minutes to review the play and make a final decision. Video clearly showed that Walton's knee was down before he lateralled the ball. It should have ended the play. Yet, the officials determined he wasn't down. They also overturned an illegal-block penalty. The touchdown stood and Miami won.

The next day, the Atlantic Coast Conference revealed their disgust for the officiating on the play. They suspended the on-field officials and the two replay booth officials for two games.

Crazy things can happen when you play "hot potato."

Corn Elder beams a giddy smile after scoring on the eight-lateral, game-ending touchdown. Elder employed his blazing speed and showed two nifty moves at midfield during his 90-yard sprint to the end zone.

GLOSSARY

CPR Acronym for cardiopulmonary resuscitation; an emergency lifesaving procedure that is performed when someone's heartbeat or breathing has stopped.

down the ball When a kicking or punting team touches the ball after the kick; downing the ball ends the play.

Hail Mary pass A long, desperate pass toward the end zone on the last play of the game or first half.

Heisman Trophy An annual award presented by the Heisman Trust to the best player in college football.

interim A temporary position.

lateral To pitch, throw, or hand off the football to someone behind you or right alongside you.

pocket The area where the offensive line tries to form a wall of protection for the quarterback.

pooch kick An intentionally short kick.

safety A play in which the team with the ball is tackled in the end zone; the other team gets two points and gets the ball kicked to them on the next play.

shotgun formation An offensive formation in which the quarterback lines up several yards behind the center.

true freshman A player who plays during his first year in college; a redshirt freshman plays the first time during his second year.

two-point conversion An option that each team always has after a touchdown; instead of a kicked extra point, the team can try to score two points by passing or running into the end zone when starting at the 2-yard line (NFL) or 3-yard line (college).

FURTHER READING

Books

Editors of *Sports Illustrated for Kids*. *Big Book of Who: Football*. New York, NY: Sports Illustrated, 2015.

Gray, Aaron Jonathan. *Football Record Breakers*. Edina, MN: ABDO Publishing, 2016.

Jacobs, Greg. *The Everything Kids' Football Book*. Fairfield, OH: Adams Media, 2014.

Van Pelt, Don, and Brian Wingate. *An Insider's Guide to Football*. New York, NY: Rosen Publishing, 2015.

Websites

NFL Rush

nflrush.com

Includes kids-oriented NFL stories, word games, quizzes, computer games, and tons of other fun stuff.

NFL Zone

sikids.com/nfl-zone

Sports Illustrated for Kids offers NFL stories that kids will enjoy, plus a Cool Stuff section, Kid Reporter, and more.

Pro-Football-Reference.com

football-reference.com

Includes statistics on every player in NFL history. For college football stats, go to sports-reference.com/cfb.

INDEX